Advance Prais
Spend & Grow

The area of finances was a real source of conflict in our marriage. We both dreaded conversations about money. One of us was a "spender" and one of us was a "saver". We needed help and found it with Gary Barnes's *Spend & Grow Rich*. Now we openly communicate about finances and our marriage has been help tremendously!

– Jim and Gloria, Colorado

Gary's *Spend & Grow Rich* helps to get to the root of what money means to you. By going through this process you will be able to set up a road map for your financial future and feel great about it!

– Rebecca, Wyoming

I have been in the banking industry for 23 years. *Spend & Grow Rich* allows you to walk away with the tools to immediately put your finances on track. Gary uses down-to-earth, easy understandable style which also addresses the emotional ways to your financial decisions. I feel this is very important because you can put all of the proper tools in place but if you do not understand why, there will never be any follow-through. Gary speaks to you from the heart.

– Barb, Colorado

I had worked in entertainment accounting for 20 years before moving to Northwest Arkansas. I found the life change to be not only personal, but financial as well. Readjusting my lifestyle has been an amazing experience but also very scary. After reading Gary Barnes's *Spend & Grow Rich* and applying the principles, I am no longer frighten of my financial future. He makes it very easy to understand and if you are serious about building a stable and rewarding financial future, Gary's step-by-step process will give you all of the tools you need to do that. Life will deal you winning and losing financial hands. It is all about maximizing the gains of limiting the losses that I found very helpful. I wish they would offer this as a mandatory course for high school seniors. I highly recommend it! Thanks Gary! Keep up the good work!

– Tina, Northwest Arkansas

Thanks Gary for sharing the gift of *Spend & Grow Rich* with all who are ready to step into their financial genius. Someone just starting could really benefit as this is brilliant and you made it so easy. I embraced a few new ideas to accelerate my path to financial freedom. Thank you!

– Lana, California

It has been about nine months since we started working through the process and now every month I can see the benefits. I never would like to receive the unexpected bills, but now at least I know that we do have money set aside for the unexpected. This is the first Christmas in 23 years that we have been married that we actually have the money set aside for gifts. This year we can fully enjoy the gift sharing with family and friends, as we know that we do not have to go into debt this Christmas season. *Spend & Grow Rich* has not only helped us use our finances but has also helped us in how we talk, respond and treat each other.

– Thomas and Martha, Colorado

I am an independent musician with an extensive background in entertainment accounting. I found the advice and material presented in Gary Barnes's *Spend & Grow Rich* to be most helpful and liberating. When you have a goal and a clear path to achieve it as set out in *Spend & Grow Rich*, the only thing left to do, is just to do it! His presentation is logical, fun and most importantly, doable. I would highly recommend *Spend & Grow Rich* to everyone looking to create a stress-free financial future. Every musician should consider the benefits of having this knowledge before spending a lot of money on the industry "experts". In the end, we are all responsible for our own "nest egg". This program gives you back the power and freedom to build it is large or small as you are willing to put the effort into it. Thanks Gary!

– D'Lorah, Arkansas

Our finances were a mess, within one month of applying *Spend & Grow Rich*, we were not only headed in the right direction, we had quite a bit of money left over each month! We even opened a savings account. Gary's spending plan is awesome! It's easy, flexible and best of all you sign it to fit your needs and goals. It takes some work and you must dedicate yourself to it, but it is magic and I promise you it works. *Spend & Grow Rich* will change the way to your finances forever.

– Greg and Jenn, Colorado

Spend & Grow Rich is comprehensive, simple, dynamic and fun. Gary teaches you how to go beyond just budgets to understanding how to make decisions about your money. He helps you learn how to talk about money, and manage your money effectively.

– John, Colorado

Spend & Grow Rich two-tiered approach gently forces individuals to recognize their needs versus their desires – and achieve both! I can't phantom anyone reaching true financial success without using this methodology to create a solid foundation. As a financial advisor, I encourage my clients to take these very steps before we begin to work on short and long-term investments. *Spend & Grow Rich* is a must-have to creating an empowered, bright future!

– Linda, Virginia

Spend & Grow Rich

The Secrets to Unlocking
the Goldmine in YOUR
Checkbook!

The Two-Tier System
A Spending Plan That
Works

Gary Barnes

ISBN: 978-0-9837630-2-4

Names and certain details of case information mentioned in this manual have been changed to protect the privacy of the people involved. However, we have attempted to convey the essence of the experience and the underlying principles as accurately as possible.

Editors: Sharon M. Barnes and Kelly C. Barnes
Designer: Jason Sornsuwan

Dedication

This is dedicated to my wife, Sharon, and my family, who have lived with a variable income for over thirty years.

Acknowledgements

I would like to thank my clients who have used the Two-Tier Spending Plan through the years. Through their feedback, they have confirmed the value of the system and have made it possible to refine it to its current state.

I would also like to thank those who have helped me in writing and producing this book. My wife Sharon Barnes, and my son Jason Sornsuwan, have been invaluable every step of the way. Mimi Hardendorf, my daughter-in-law Kelly Barnes were also kind enough to read the manuscript and give suggestions for its improvement.

I would also like to thank my readers, for their desire for a better life, for their risk-taking ability and their choice to invest in Spend & Grow Rich.

Thanks to all.

Contents

1

Introduction

Congratulations! You have invested in Spend & Grow Rich the Two-Tier System, which can help you take control of your own financial life. You have taken your first step in creating your own Financial Destiny!

Why Spend & Grow Rich?

Because that's exactly what we do. I'll be sharing common sense tools you can use to transform your personal finances. Your true income and expenses will appear, and your stress around finances will disappear, as if by magic!

By following the strategies that are found in the Spend & Grow Rich System, you will be able to eliminate the stress around your personal finances! By implementing the Two-Tier System—by creating and following your own Spending Plan—your money will go farther, you will have less anxiety about your money, and you will have increased purchasing power. By reaching your financial goals, you will create financial security in your own life!

Please complete the full Spend & Grow Rich process before deciding whether or not it will work for you. I originally developed what I now call my two-tier system to use for my personal spending plan. I have also used it with my financial planning clients for over twenty-five years.

> *Most people spend about 110% of what they earn.*

During these twenty-five plus years in the financial industry, I have found a common thread: Most people spend about 110% of what they earn. I have clients that earn as little as $20,000 per year to clients that earn well over $1,000,000 per year. At times, all of them work hard to make ends meet.

How to Be True Rich!

We all spend or allocate 100% of the dollars that come into our possession every month.

Some people Spend and Grow Rich, some spend and just get by, and some people spend and grow poor. I have found three factors that make a dramatic difference in the final result.

> *Some people Spend and Grow Rich, some spend and just get by, and some people spend and grow poor.*

They are:

1. The True Rich are savers. They pay themselves first. The baseline has always been to save at least 10% of your income.

2. The True Rich spend only present dollars and not future dollars, except in extreme emergencies (which does not include routine or predictable expenses that we have not planned for). We are literally giving away

> *The True Rich are savers. They pay themselves first.*

our wealth when we make interest payments on loans and credit cards.

3. The True Rich plan and track their finances. They know how much comes in and where they spend it. They have financial goals, both long-term and short-term, and they follow their plans to make their goals happen. Rather than just working for their money, their money is truly working for them.

When I say, True Rich, I am speaking about people who don't wear their wealth for all to see. They are more focused on the freedoms their money gives them, instead of the status it gives them.

> *The True Rich are more focused on the freedoms their money gives them, instead of the status it gives them.*

Money gives the True Rich the freedom from worry about paying bills or meeting their living expenses. It gives them freedom to invest. It gives them freedom to make contributions to their chosen causes. It gives them freedom to live their lives the way they choose, rather than making every decision by the dollar. It gives them the freedom to do what they want when they want. Spend & Grow Rich teaches you essential skills you need if you want to be True Rich. You may or may not desire a big house, an expensive car or a lavish lifestyle. You may desire a simple life, without financial worries. Whatever it is that you desire, Spend & Grow Rich can show you how to get it.

What is it that YOU Desire From Your Money?

Take a few minutes now to think about your reasons for seeking a different financial destiny in your life, the results that you are looking for in your finances, and the impact this will have on your life. It is crucial for you to know why you desire this.

One principle of success in any venture is, "If the why is strong enough, the how doesn't matter." In other words, if you know why you are doing something, and your reasons are compelling enough, you will surmount any obstacle you

> *If the why is strong enough, the how doesn't matter.*

encounter to achieve the success you seek. So, find a quiet place and take a few minutes to consider the following four questions and write your answers.

1. What freedoms will you have when you no longer worry about your finances?

2. Why do you want to change your financial situation?

3. What results are you looking for from your money?

4. How will this impact your life? What will be different or better about your life as a result?

How to Get the Most Bang From Your Buck

To get the most out of your efforts, I recommend that you make a copy of the previous questions, which can also be found in Appendix A-1, and post it where you can see it often. You may find it helpful to review it when you sit down to work with your Two-Tier Spending Plan. You may find it helpful to review it if you get discouraged with the process of change. You can also review it if you slip back into old habits. Many people find it helpful to read it aloud daily for the first few months of implementing their Two-Tier Spending Plan.

Your answers to the questions can help you to remember why you are doing this as well as what results you expect from making these changes in your life. Remembering why you are making and fol-

What freedoms will you have when you no longer worry about your finances?

lowing your Two-Tier Spending Plan can encourage you to continue and remind you that Financial Freedom can happen in your life, too! As Napoleon Hill said, "Whatever the mind of man [and woman] can conceive and believe, it can achieve!"

Ben and Sally were referred to me by a family therapist to work with them on their financial situation. They both made substantial incomes from their jobs but never seemed to have enough money to go around. They were both feeling very guilty about their situation and yet they were using guilt against each other about their finances. They desperately wanted to stop arguing about money and to start to enjoy the life their money could bring them.

They implemented the two-tier system and started to see immediate results. Three months into the process they took a vacation to Hawaii and when they returned they called me to say they did everything they wanted to and they had spent less than what they had planned. The best part they said was that they were able to spend the money on their vacation guilt free!

> *The best part they said was that they were able to spend the money on their vacation guilt free!*

Spend & Grow Rich provides you with tools to take control of your financial life. The process of establishing your personal "Two-Tier Spending Plan" will give you a visual picture of where your money goes every month. We all have cash flow—some positive, some negative. When you follow this system, you can take your finances out of negative cash flow and into positive cash flow. Is having magic in your finances what you dream of and are ready for? Then let's begin!

2

Getting Started

What is Your Starting Point?

As we get started, I believe we need to ask the question, "How did I (or we) get into my (our) present financial condition?" Most of us never received any education in school, or from our families about how to handle our finances.

Somehow, when we graduate from high school or college and get into our first jobs, we're supposed to automatically know how to handle our finances, create a budget, spend our money wisely

> *How did I (or we) get into my (our) present financial condition?*

and save for our futures. Without having any formal background, or at the very least, maybe one class in school, we are not prepared to handle the decision making process that life requires of us.

We look at easy terms and the things that we want and, as Americans, we want all those things now.

There is a phenomenon that I refer to as "New Rich." This can happen whenever you have an unexpected amount of money that comes into your possession. This can happen when you are self-employed or get paid by commission and close a big sale, or it can happen when you receive a promotion or higher-paying job. This often happens when you first enter the workplace and go from zero or minimum wage income to an income that is much larger. It can even happen before that. I was amazed when my oldest son went to college, and one of the required registration stops was to sign up for a credit card with an instant credit limit of $1,000! As a parent, I was unaware of it until the first bill came and my son called me to ask how he was supposed to make the payment!

That is just one example of how our society handles credit. We look at easy terms and the things that we want and, as Americans, we want all those things *now*. I know I have. We don't want to wait for them and we don't want to plan and save for them. And so we enter the "rat race." We work to pay our bills, rather than working toward what we want in life. If we don't put together a solid foundation to build upon, then we're building our house upon sand. Anything that comes along—any emergency, any unexpected expense—can truly devastate our finances. We find ourselves always catching up instead of getting ahead.

What is Money?

Money is neither good nor bad; it's neutral. The power and importance that money takes on is what we give it. If this is true, why do so many of us feel so much negative

> *Money is neither good nor bad; it's neutral.*

emotion about money? I believe it comes down to control. The more a person feels, and is, in control of their money, the more neutral or even positive money becomes.

Many of us have been raised with the concept that money is the root of all evil. The true Biblical text is "the love of money is a root of all kinds of evil" (I Timothy 6:10, NIV). While money is not the most important thing in our lives, it ranks right up there in the top with food, water and air. One of the wisest men of all time, King Solomon, also said, "Money is the answer to everything" (Ecclesiastes 10:19, NIV). Without adequate resources, we are at the mercy of those around us that take pity on us or those that are waiting in the wings to take advantage of us with high interest rates, which enslave us to a life that is not fulfilled.

Money is only a unit of measure. Simply put, money is the way we exchange what we have for what others have that we want. We just happen to use paper currency and metal coins to exchange for goods and services. We could use livestock, seashells, or anything else the community places value on.

The Impact of Plastic Money

In recent years, we have been using plastic (credit cards) more and more as a substitute for actual money. Now we are moving to Direct Banking. Our paychecks are electronically deposited into our bank accounts; we pay our bills and make purchases electronically, and we never even see or touch any tangible money. This separation from physical dollars has taken away much of the pain of spending. It also removes us further from the reality of what we have to spend and from balancing our accounts.

I have a friend Carl that refers to his credit card availability as "my money that I haven't spent yet." The problem here is that it's not "his" money. It's someone else's money that he has access to that

> *The separation from physical dollars has taken away much of the pain of spending.*

over time will cost more of "his" money to use. He is literally making someone else Rich!

The main purpose of this book is to empower you regarding your finances, so that you can live a truly fulfilled life. It doesn't matter if you have started out and have made some mistakes in the past. It doesn't matter if you're in your teens, twenties, fifties, or later on in retirement. It is never too late to get a handle on and take control of your finances

With Spend & Grow Rich, You'll Make a Spending Plan, Not a Budget

In Spend & Grow Rich, you will not use a budget; instead, we will help you develop your own personal Two-Tier Spending Plan. People don't like budgets. Many have tried budgets and failed. Others don't know how to make a budget adjustable. Their budget is set in concrete, and when people deviate from them, they feel like they have failed, or they feel guilty or ashamed, and they give up on the whole thing. Guilt has no payoff, so we don't go there.

> *It is never too late to get a handle on and take control of your finances.*

People do love to spend money. Therefore, we will help you develop a Two-Tier Spending Plan that's designed around you and is flexible, while it is also tailored to your needs, your life, and your goals.

If you came to my financial planning office to consult with me, I'd be asking you questions and listening to your answers. I have some questions for you now. Please take the time and effort to think about these questions, write out your own answers, and discuss them with your partner, if you have one. For easy reference, these five questions are also printed in Appendix A-2.

1. What does money mean to you?
2. How do you feel about money? What are your emotions around money?
3. Do you think that money is good, bad, or indifferent? How, and why?
4. How much money is enough for you?
5. How will you know when you have enough money?

Money is an Emotional Topic

One of the biggest obstacles to improving our financial lives, or making any kind of improvement in our lives, is our emotions when we deal with money.

We often feel scared, guilty, ashamed, sad, angry, or something else just as uncomfortable. Remember that guilt, shame, or blame has no payoff.

Feel it, and let it go. Forgive yourself and your partner for any bad choices or mistakes you have made. Anger can be turned into creative energy to help you make the necessary changes to feel good about your finances and yourself. Do not anchor yourself in the past mistakes you or your partner have made or in your ignorance or errors in judgment; instead, harness your emotions and the energy in them to help you move toward your goals.

> *Remember that guilt, shame, or blame has no payoff.*

Your Road Map

In preparing for your Spend & Grow Rich Two-Tier Spending Plan, we ask that you look at your personal spending habits, your debt structure, and the decisions that you have made around money. We will also give you an opportunity to personally design your desired outcome. Since we live in the most prosperous nation in history, opportunities are all around us. We simply have to look at our goals and set up a road map—a specifically designed plan to accomplish these goals. These three questions, also found in Appendix A-3, will help you create that road map.

1. What is it that you would like to see in a "perfect" world? To put it another way, what do you day-dream about financially?

2. What are your financial goals? Be as specific as you can.

> *We simply have to look at our goals and set up a road map.*

3. Looking into your future, where would you like your final financial destination to be? For example, where would you like to live, what type of home would you like to live in, what charities would you like to support, what schools would you like your children to attend?

3

First Steps

Your First Steps Toward Financial Control in Your Life

Before starting on any trip, it is helpful to know where you are going and where you are starting. Step 1 of the Two-Tier Spending Plan is to look at your personal finances—where money has come from and where you have spent your money on a monthly basis.

To do this, we recommend that you start with your check register. If you use one of the software programs like Quicken or Microsoft Money, print out an Itemized Category Report. This enables you to see the various categories and where money has been spent over the last three months. Make sure to categorize all of your expenditures and then add them up. While you are gathering information, it is important to also look for those expenses that only occur quarterly, semi-annually, or annually. Add those into your totals as well.

> *What we want to determine is a monthly average of how much money you need to pay all of your ongoing expenses.*

What we want to determine is a monthly average of how much money you need to pay all of your ongoing expenses. Finally, divide the total by three to get a monthly average. You will need as accurate a total for your income and expenses as you can get, because these totals will be used as the basis for your whole Two-Tier Spending Plan. Take this information and transfer it to the Tier 1 Worksheet, located in Appendix C-1. We will cover this more in depth in a short time; for now, simply list all of your expenses.

This process may be somewhat difficult. Many times we don't want to look at things as they really are. This might be because we are afraid of what we may find out. We may be afraid to discover how much money is going to some areas, or how much money we have not kept track of. If we know we don't have enough money for something we want to buy, we feel more responsible than if we don't know. When we don't know, we can pretend we have more than we do and deal with the consequences later.

Knowledge Empowers Us

Knowing where we are is essential to finding a path to take us where we want to go. Sometimes, we discover things are worse than we thought. Other times, we find out that they are not as bad as we were afraid.

Either way, we need to forge ahead with this process. You may find surprises in doing this research. There will be things that you think you have spent money on that you haven't;

> *Knowing where we are is essential to finding a path to take us where we want to go.*

you may also find things that you have spent more on than you realized. The information that you have gathered builds the foundation for the accountability phase of building a Two-Tier Spending Plan that will serve you for a lifetime.

> *You will experience discomfort while you build new habits.*

There is a little bad news. You will experience discomfort while you build new habits and a new relationship with money. It will also take effort on your part. My goal is not to try to make you into an accountant or financial planner. My goal is to give you the tools that you need (and I hope that you want them as well) to once and for all take control of your financial life.

You Are (Already) a Millionaire

It is not how much money that you make that gives you the financial freedom that you desire. Implementing a system that helps you maximize the power of the dollars that come into your control creates financial freedom. All of us, even those who make $25,000 a year, earn a million dollars over a

40-year working life! If you knew you were a millionaire, how would that change your financial decisions? Would that help you make a better plan? Would it help you follow through on your plan? Now you know that you are a millionaire! You can refer to Appendix D to see just how much you will earn over your lifetime.

I have had clients whose income was well into the high six figures, and who still worried about bouncing checks to the grocery store every pay day. My observations have shown

> *If you knew you were a millionaire, how would that change your financial decisions?*

that, in the United States, we have a tendency to live about 10% above our means. That's the average; not a happy one, but it's the norm.

This brings us to another obstacle in your path. In order to change your financial situation, you will have to buck the system. You will have to step out and be different. From childhood, most of us have wanted to fit it, to belong. So we go with the crowd, we do what everyone around us is doing. It takes courage to step out and be different. It takes valuing yourself and your life enough to make the effort required to swim upstream, against the current. This is a good time to review the list that you wrote earlier concerning why you want Financial Security in your life, and to add to that list if possible. To review, what are the results you are looking for, what are the freedoms you are seeking, and why?

Balanced Spending

You may be encouraged to know that I also have clients who have had very modest incomes during their working life and have amassed a sizable amount of wealth by their late fifties or early sixties.

They have mastered the art of balancing their spending. They have used their monies wisely and have accumulated wealth that will serve them well into their retirement years. They did this without having to sacrifice the enjoyment of the accumulation years. I have made a study of the differences between these people and those who are always

> *They have mastered the art of balancing their spending.*

in financial stress. I will be sharing these differences with you.

These differences and the way money is allocated both before and after monthly and necessary expenditures is the foundation of the Two-Tier Spending Plan. The way that this system came about is that I have never had a predictable salary—a set amount that would be coming into the household. Therefore, I had to come up with some way of designing a plan that would work for us. Some months would be much larger in income than others, and there was no real way of designing a traditional budget that was going to work. Hence, the Two-Tier Spending Plan was created. I hope that you will find it as helpful as I and my clients have.

Make a Plan Together With Your Partner

If you are married or have a significant other who has his or her finances combined with yours, it is very important that you both be involved in gathering the information and in the decision-making, implementation and accountability phases of the Two-Tier Spending Plan. You're going to have different spending habits and different perspectives on many issues. Opposites do attract, and normally you have a saver, or someone that doesn't have a big need to spend money, married or connected to a person that has more of a need to spend and enjoys shopping, etc. This, by the way, does not always mean the woman. I have seen it with both males and females.

> *Opposites do attract, so often you have a saver connected to a shopper.*

If you'll go through this process together, discussing at a non-emotional time, you will avoid many emotional or heated discussions around finances later on. Money is the number one reason that people identify as ultimately leading to divorce in the United States. Spend & Grow Rich is designed to help eliminate money as a source of conflict and stress in your relationships.

If you will build your Two-Tier Spending Plan at a time when you don't have to make immediate decisions, then you will find that when dollars do come into your possession, you can put it against the framework of your Two-Tier Spending Plan, and you'll find that your money goes much farther, and actually does what you want it to do.

Agreeing on some ground rules for communication about your finances can be very helpful. Good rules to start with are: no guilt slinging, no blaming, no if-only, and stick to the subject.

It is especially important to pay attention to when and where you work on this. I don't recommend that you do it when you are hungry, tired, stressed or hurried. I don't recommend that you do it at night. I do recommend that you make an appointment with each other, so that you can both be at your best to do this, and so you can have uninterrupted time to do it. I also recommend that you take your phone off the hook or, at least, let your calls go to voice mail during your scheduled Two-Tier Planning Time.

> *Spend & Grow Rich is designed to help eliminate money as a source of conflict and stress in your relationships.*

Assets and Liabilities

Before you can start to eliminate your debt, it is important to know your monthly income and total assets before moving onto debt elimination. The following questions will help you to identify your monthly income as well as your assets. For your convenience, these questions can also be found in Appendix B-1, and the income sources portion is also a component of Tier 1, which we shall cover shortly.

1. List your income sources. Include your salary, commissions, bonuses, etc.

   Income Type   Amount

   _____   _____

   _____   _____

   _____   _____

   _____   _____

   _____   _____

   Total _____

2. List all of your financial assets. Consider such items as stocks, bonds, art, collectibles, cash, real estate, retirement accounts, etc.

Item   Value

_____   _____

_____   _____

_____   _____

_____   _____

_____   _____

_____   _____

_____   _____

Total _____

3. List your intangible assets. This could include things like your desire for a better life, your courage, your determination, your family and friends, your health, your skills, etc.

Now that you know your total income and assets, you can look to your liabilities. When taking inventory of where you are, it is critical to list all of your creditors, the current balance on each account, the percentage rate that you're paying, and the monthly payment that you make. List these so you can add up the total of all of the balances and the total of the monthly payments. We'll use this later in developing your monthly Two-Tier Spending Plan. Refer to the

Debt Inventory, found in Appendix B-2 to complete this task. This is a good time to remind yourself that you didn't gather your debts overnight and you won't liquidate your debts overnight, either. Later in the process, we'll show you a systematic way to become debt-free.

Congratulations! "Beginning is Half Done!" By creating your foundational belief systems, you are now ready to create the structure you will need to implement your Two-Tier Spending Plan.

> *You have surmounted the biggest hurdles: inertia and leaving your comfort zone.*

You have surmounted the biggest hurdles: inertia and leaving your comfort zone! You have been willing to look at and discover the truth about where you are. This is the first and biggest step toward the freedoms that you desire, deserve and will achieve as you move through the steps of the Two-Tier Spending Plan. You are well on your way to creating Financial Riches in your life!

4

Creating Your Two-Tier Spending Plan

Your Tier 1 Foundation

In developing a monthly spending plan, we not only have to account for items that are paid on a monthly basis but also those that are paid on quarterly, semi-annual, and annual billing cycles. Take the time now to double-check the Tier 1 Worksheet, found in Appendix C-1, which you completed earlier. Remember that the more accurately you complete this task, the better end-result you'll achieve.

Include ALL of Your Expenses

By accounting for all regular and especially odd-timing expenses, the months when they come due will not catch you off guard and throw off your spending plan. It is extremely important for you to take the time necessary to account for all of your expenses and needs for your spending plan to be totally effective.

Your Tier 1 Worksheet, or Tier 1 Template, shows an outline of the general categories in which most people have expenses. I have also given you space at the bottom of the worksheet for additional categories that you can customize to your particular needs. When you list your credit accounts such as credit cards, use the minimum monthly payment in Tier 1. I'll show you how to reduce and eliminate your debt in Tier 2. Hint: In Tier 1, the key goal is to have the lowest total possible. You know that when this amount of income comes in, all of your basic needs are met. It is a great feeling of control when this happens.

In developing a list of your basic needs, there are categories such as gifts, clothing, and recreation. If you didn't spend much money in these areas the world wouldn't end. Therefore, put in a small dollar value in these categories. Rest assured, this doesn't mean you won't be able to spend more in these areas—it will be included in Tier 2.

I highly recommend having an allowance for you and your partner, if you have one. The amount doesn't have to be large, but these dollars allow for guilt-free spending without needing anyone else's, or your own, consent.

> *I highly recommend having an allowance for you and your partner, if you have one.*

This process was especially disturbing for Tom and Beverly. Tom was a corporate executive and Beverly was a CPA. They seemed to always have challenge in making the money they received stretch for all of the needs of the family. When they created their tier 1 needs it became apparent that 29% of their gross income was going to their young sons hockey endeavors. While this expense was not wrong per se, it was putting extraordinary pressure on the financial well-being of the family. They initially wanted me to come up with a magical solution, but I reminded them about economics 101. There are only two basic solutions to having a balanced financial life. One is to receive more money and the other is to lower expenses. Tom and Beverly logically already knew this, but they had allowed their emotions to make their financial decisions. By making their finances visible they were able to reallocate and adjust their spending habits for their desired outcome.

Two Tiers of Spending

Now comes a very special step in building your Two-Tier Spending Plan: creating Tier 2, the unique feature of the Two-Tier Spending Plan. While Tier 1 accounts for all necessary expenses, Tier 2 allocates the income left over and not used in Tier 1.

By making their finances visible they were able to reallocate and adjust their spending habits for their desired outcome.

The main difference between the Tiers is the way you relate to expenses. In Tier 1, a dollar amount is allocated for each category. The assumption is made that your income is sufficient to meet at least the Tier 1 basic expenses. In Tier 2, however, a percentage amount is allocated. For Tier 2 to be balanced, the total of the percentages must equal 100. By combining Tier 1 and Tier 2, you guarantee that you will not spend more than your total income in any given month.

Tier 2 should not contain more than 10 categories. If you give your categories small percentage values because you have many categories, you run the risk of putting only a few dollars in each category and not feeling like you are accomplishing your desired goals. Tier 2 can duplicate some of the categories in Tier 1. For example, you may have clothing budgeted in Tier 1 for general monthly clothing expenditures. You also need to plan for clothing replacement and updating your wardrobe(s), so you will have a clothing category in both Tiers.

By integrating the Two-Tier Spending Plan into your personal financial plan, you will guarantee that each category will have some money allocated to it on a monthly basis, provided there are excess dollars. The months that your income is less, there will be less in each of these categories; the months that your income is more, you will have proportionately more in each category. No category gets ignored, and all go up and down with your income. It is simple to implement this, once you have your Tiers in place. Appendices C-1 through C-4 contain Tier 1 and Tier 2 Worksheets to help guide you as you create your own Two-Tier Spending Plan.

How to Pay Off Your Debts

As promised, here's a systematic way to pay off outstanding indebtedness, such as credit cards. To do this, make a category for Debt Reduction in Tier 2. Refer to your Debt Inventory, found in Appendix B-2, and identify the debt that has the highest interest rate being paid on it. Combine the Tier 1 amount for that debt with the percentage allocated to Debt Reduction in Tier 2. Doing this, you pay off your highest interest rate account first.

When that first account has been completely paid off, you allocate the amount that you had been paying in Tier 1 to that debt and the percentage from Tier 2 for Debt Reduction to the debt with the next highest interest rate. You then continue this process until all of your debts are paid off. This may seem overwhelming, but this systematic process will help you become debt-free more quickly. Remember, your financial freedom becomes that much closer each time you eliminate your debt obligations.

An example of this is when you have three credit cards that you want to pay off. Referring to Appendix B-3, you will find that, in the sample, the Chase credit card has the highest interest rate. Therefore, you will get the most financial return by paying it off first. In this sample, June is the first month that you are using your Two-Tier Spending Plan. In June, you would make your minimum monthly payment of $19.00. At the end of June you also have $189.40 in your debt reduction category in Tier 2. So, in July, you would send Chase a payment of $208.40, which includes the June Tier 2 and July Tier 1 amounts. When the Chase card is completely paid off, you move on to the card with the next highest interest rate, which would be the Capital One credit card, and you repeat the process. You will be pleasantly surprised at how quickly your debt will disappear using this method.

With the goal of paying off your debts, it's a given that you do not add to them. Using your Two-Tier

Spending Plan, you will pay for your expenses from your designated categories, and you will not need to add to your debt. By keeping this goal and your reasons for implementing your Two-Tier Spending Plan in front of you, you will change your spending habits, and thus create Financial Magic in your own life!

You will be pleasantly surprised at how quickly your debt will disappear using this method.

In this way you are reducing your debt in a systematic way and having the greatest positive impact on your finances by eliminating the highest interest rates first. When all your debt is paid, this will free up capital to be put into other categories in Tier 1 and Tier 2 in your Two-Tier Spending Plan.

Take Time to Celebrate!

By creating Tiers 1 and 2, you have achieved a grand accomplishment that calls for celebration and congratulations! It's time to *celebrate your accomplishments*! I highly recommend that you recognize and celebrate each step along the way. Make small celebrations for small steps, and bigger celebrations for bigger steps and achievements. The following three questions are to help you "brainstorm" celebration options and can be found in Appendix A-4.

1. How would you like to celebrate? What would be a small celebration for you?

2. What would be a large celebration for you?

3. What celebration can you have right now that will help you acknowledge and congratulate yourself for the difficult work that you have done so far?

It's time to celebrate your accomplishments!

5

Tracking Your Spending and Your Excess

After establishing your foundation in Step 1 and creating your Two-Tier Spending Plan in Step 2, you are now ready for Step 3, which is the implementation of your new Spending Plan. This can be the most intimidating of all the steps. If you find it difficult to do this, just remember that we anticipated this in the introduction, so you are prepared. You made a copy of pages eight and nine (or of Appendix A-1), so you can easily remind yourself of why you are executing the Two-Tier Spending Plan. If you find it difficult, this is a prime time to take this page out and read it aloud to yourself.

Tracking Options

To track your spending and your excess, you have a number of choices:

1. Track manually. You can use a ledger book to record your monthly income and expenses and then transfer unused dollar amounts in Tier 2 to a second ledger. This will obviously take more time but can be used if other options are not available.

2. Use accounting software. I recommend the use of Quicken Home & Business to my clients, which I use as well. Microsoft Money and other programs are readily available also. Any one of these programs allows you to create categories and subcategories and transfer money from one account to another. One of the reasons I like these programs is that they eliminate all of the math errors. Finding input errors is also quick and easy because you're comparing your entries with a paper statement from your bank. In addi-

tion, once they are set up, most people can balance their checkbooks and monitor their Two-Tier Spending Plan in just 30 to 45 minutes per month.

3. Use a professional. There is a misconception that only the wealthy use bookkeepers, accountants and CPA's. This is simply not true. Some people find it beneficial to hire a professional to do their tracking for them. If financial tracking is not your strength, or if your time or energy is limited, this could be your best option. You still have to do Steps 1 and 2, for no one can determine your goals or specify your Tiers; however, Step 3 is the mechanical aspect of the Two-Tier Spending Plan and can be outsourced. You would provide your monthly information to the professional and he or she would provide you with a statement showing your Spending Plan results for that month.

Keep Tier 2 Money Separate

One question that often arises is, "When you have excess money left over in a category—when there is less or no expenditure in that category—where should those extra dollars be kept?" I recommend that you open a separate savings account for your Tier 2 excess. Every month you then transfer the excess money from that category into your Tier 2 Savings Account. This account is defined by each of your Tier 2 categories, so the money is then allocated accordingly.

If you plan to track the extra dollars manually, we have provided a Tier 2 Worksheet, which can be found in Appendix C-3. It is also easy to track these dollars using computer software, or you can work with a professional. I recommend that you make this step as simple and uncomplicated as possible. I find that my clients who make it too complicated become discouraged and don't continue with the Two-Tier Spending Plan.

You may be tempted to spend the excess dollars, but if you will save these funds in their given categories, you will have the money available when it is needed. You will already be prepared when your car needs to be repaired, when Christmas comes and you're ready to go out and buy presents, when your child's shoes sprout holes, or when your favorite clothing store has its annual sale. You will have the money to spend, without the guilt. You will not worry where the money will come from or what bill not to pay in order to meet this need. By transferring those dollars to your Tier 2 Savings Account, this also gets the money out of your checking account, so you are less likely to spend those dollars in an area that you had not included in your Two-Tier Spending Plan.

Set Aside Reserve Funds

In Tier 2, one category I always recommend is the Reserve Account, or Emergency Fund. I am often asked how much money people should allocate to this category. My answer is, "That depends." You may get frustrated with that answer, but it truly does depend on the needs and the size and the personality of the household. Each of my clients has a different number that is acceptable for them, and when they have that amount of money in their reserve account, they relax, knowing that they have cash to solve most, if not all, of their emergency needs.

Generally speaking, I recommend that people ultimately build up their Reserve Account to an amount equal to three months of Tier 1 expenses if they are employed, or at least six months of Tier 1 expenses if they are self-employed or business owners. This amount will accumulate over time, since only a percentage of your excess will go towards your Reserve Account each month. It is important to note that this Reserve Account is not a separate bank account but is one of many "sub-accounts" or categories within your Tier 2 Savings Account. While having multiple accounts is possible, it is often very confusing, and it is unnecessary.

After building up your Reserve Account to the appropriate amount, as described above, you do not continue to add to this category. Since you completed or filled this category and reached your goal, your further excess dollars are reallocated to other, or new, categories within your Tier-Two Spending Plan.

For example, you choose to allocate 10% of your excess dollars to your Reserve Account in Tier 2. If you want to have $10,000 saved in your Reserve Account, then you allocate the appropriate amount—10%—each month. When your Tier 2 Savings Account has $10,000 allocated to your Reserve Account category, that category is considered closed. The 10% that was being allocated to your Reserve Account is now reallocated to other categories. These categories may already be established, or you can create new categories altogether.

Again, the thing to remember is that this Spending Plan is totally flexible. It is meant to flex and grow with your circumstances. Please do not complicate Tier 2. You simply want to see where the money is coming from, and where the money is going.

> *Remember is that this Spending Plan is totally flexible.*

How to Handle Emergencies

With your Two-Tier Spending Plan in place, you are already prepared when an expense comes up. For example, when you have a home repair and have accumulated money in that category in your Tier 2 Savings Account, you can transfer the dollars that are needed to your checking account. Therefore, you do not put your home repair expense on a credit card like you may have done before you established your Two-Tier Spending Plan.

Another situation that sometimes arises while you begin to establish and maintain your Two-Tier Spending Plan is that you can have an expense come up in a category, but there is not enough money in that category to pay that expense. An example would be if you have $200 accumulated for Auto Repair in your Tier 2 Savings Account, and you have a $500 repair bill on your car. Including the $200 allocated to Auto Repair, you have a total of $600 in your entire Savings Account. Since you have $600 total in your Tier 2 Savings Account, you can borrow the $300 additional dollars from the other categories to pay the remainder of the repair bill. Taking the $200 from your Auto Repair category and $300 from the other categories leaves you with $100 in your Savings Account overall. You would show a negative balance of $300 in your Auto Repair category, and you would also show money owed to the categories that you borrowed from.

What you do is borrow the money from yourself, and then pay that money back to yourself in the following months. Borrowing money from the other categories in Tier 2 is preferable, since you do not want to add to your current debt. As you allocate money to your Tier 2 Saving Account in future months, it will not go to the Auto Repair category; instead, it will go to the categories you borrowed from. The money will not go to Auto Repair until you have paid back the categories that you borrowed from.

The whole idea here is to stop paying current expenses with credit. By not going further into debt, you are taking control of your finances and moving further along the road to becoming debt-free. Appendix C-3, your Tier 2 Template, will help you establish your tracking and allocation of excess dollars.

> *The whole idea here is to stop paying current expenses with credit.*

6

The Future is Now!

Here's What You Have Done

We have come to the end of the process. You have accomplished a great deal, including, but certainly not limited to, the following:

- You have established an understanding of how and why you spend your money.

- You have established goals, dreams, and desires for your financial future.

- You've gone through Step 1 for yourself, your family or your business, and you have established where you are financially and how you got there.

- You have created your own personalized Two-Tier Spending Plan to implement.

- You have taken the time to establish all of your basic needs, and you are now aware of how much money must come in for you to complete Tier 1.

- You have created a reserve system that allocates excess dollars, so you can pay for future expenses.

- You have a way of accumulating wealth from the money that flows through your checkbook every month.

This process will enable you to take control of your financial destiny.

My challenge to you is to use the Two-Tier Spending Plan for a minimum of six months.

My challenge to you is to use the Two-Tier Spending Plan for a minimum of six months. Establish your system and do not change it for three months. After three months, look back, reevaluate your categories, see which ones need adjusting, and then continue for the next three months. If you will do that, after a six-month period, you will have established a brand new habit, you will have gained control, and you will have truly created Financial Riches in your own life!

Let's Look to the Future

One of my major goals is to help people change the direction of their financial lives, starting with directing their own financial destiny. Then they are able to help their children start their financial lives off right. By giving the children a foundation and a track to run on early, they will not have to break all the bad habits that we had, for they will have avoided these habits altogether.

You can create a miniature version of the Two-Tier Spending Plan for your children when they are young. The sooner children understand the use

> *By giving the children a foundation and a track to run on early, they will not have to break all the bad habits that we had.*

of money, the better prepared they'll be to handle it when they go out on their own. They will not experience many of the hardships, heartaches and challenges that most, if not all, Americans face today.

My mission is to give financial control back to the individual. That is partially accomplished by helping you structure your financial life in a very magical way. I am excited for you and very proud of you for going through this process. While I have kept this system as simple as possible, I realize that the math and tracking aspects can be intimidating or difficult. Rest assured, however, that after following your Two-Tier Spending Plan for six months, you will have created new habits and will have taken control of your financial life.

Congratulations! You have completed the steps to establish your own Two-Tier Spending Plan! You have come, not to the end, but to the beginning of a grand new life, a life full of Financial Riches!

Stories! Please Share Your Stories!

I hope to hear stories of what this program has done in your life, and someday to have the opportunity to meet you. As you develop and implement your own Two-Tier Spending Plan, please email me with both your questions and your results at Gary@ GaryBarnesInternational.com. Welcome to your new reality.

Janet is a widow whose husband did not share any personal financial information with her during their marriage and raising of their children. She did not participate in balancing their checkbook or the family financial plans or records. He died in his early fifties, leaving her with two teenage sons. She had little knowledge or ability to know what to do with her assets and liabilities or how to manage it all. We worked together to develop a Two-Tier Spending Plan. I worked with her until she learned how to plan, track her spending, and balance her own accounts. Today, she is fully capable of handling her finances and is enjoying a life that, a few years ago, she only dreamed about.

Patti is in her late thirties, in the medical profession, and divorced with no children. She felt like money was controlling her and, even though she was earning a great wage, wasn't seeing many tangible results. One of the beliefs we uncovered was an "all or nothing" belief that manifested itself in how she managed her personal debt. She allowed her debt to grow, and then her discomfort pushed her to try to pay off all of the debt at once. This financial roller coaster ride was wearing her out. By understanding the process to eliminate her debt, she now has more cash flow every month; she also implemented a debt reduction program that will make her debt-free. By taking control of her income, she has even reduced the amount of hours she works.

Ben and Sue are in their mid forties, and all of their children are out of the house. She is a medical professional, he is in transportation, and they have a combined income of about $125,000.00 per year. It was tax time when we first met. Their biggest frustration was after making good salaries and paying taxes, they had nothing to show for it year after year. The first step they took was to implement the Financial Magic Two-Tier Spending Plan. When we added up all of the expenses that were needed to cover Tier 1, the total was around $47,000.00. That meant that, after paying taxes, approximately $78,000.00 was being spent, but where and how they had no idea. By completing and implementing Tier 2, they now accumulate $10,000.00—$15,000.00 in a long-term program. They purchased a new home and still have extra cash to help their kids and to pamper their grandchildren.

And now the question is, what will your story be?

Guidelines to Your Appendices:

How to Maximize Their Use

The following appendices are to help guide you through the process of creating and implementing your Two-Tier Spending Plan. Use them later as a reference to see where you're going and how far you've already come. It is often helpful to copy them and keep them where you will see them often, such as in your day planners, on your mirror in the bathroom, or on the refrigerator. Doing so will help keep your dreams alive.

The Appendices are organized according to content. Section A contains the questions you answered in developing your Two-Tier Spending Plan, Section B has the list of your Assets and your Debt Inventory, Section C is the Worksheets for Tier 1 and Tier 2, and Section D contains a chart of what you will make in a lifetime.

The Appendices are subdivided as follows:

- Appendix A-1: Your Reasons for Seeking Financial Magic
- Appendix A-2: Your Feelings About Money
- Appendix A-3: Your Financial Roadmap
- Appendix A-4: Celebrate!
- Appendix B-1: Your Assets
- Appendix B-2: Debt Inventory—Template
- Appendix B-3: Debt Inventory—Sample
- Appendix C-1: Monthly Income and Tier 1 Expenses—Template
- Appendix C-2: Monthly Income and Tier 1 Expenses—Sample
- Appendix C-3: Tier 2 Expense Categories— Template

- Appendix C-4: Tier 2 Expense Categories—
  Sample
- Appendix D: You Are a Millionaire!

A-1

Your Reasons for Seeking Financial Magic

1. What freedoms will you have when you no longer worry about your finances?

_____

_____

_____

_____

2. Why do you want to change your financial situation?

_____

_____

_____

_____

3. What results are you looking for from your money?

_____

_____

_____

_____

4. How will this impact your life? What will be different or better about your life as a result?

_____

_____

_____

_____

A-2

Your Feelings About Money

1. What does money mean to you?

_____

_____

_____

_____

_____

2. How do you feel about money? What are your emotions around money?

_____

_____

_____

3. Do you think that money is good, bad, or indifferent? How, and why?

_____

_____

_____

4. How much money is enough for you?

_____

_____

_____

5. How will you know when you have enough money?

_____

_____

_____

A-3

Your Financial Roadmap

1. What is it that you would like to see in a "perfect" world? To put it another way, what do you daydream about financially?

_____

_____

_____

_____

_____

2. What are your financial goals? Be as specific as you can.

_____

_____

_____

_____

_____

3. Looking into your future, where would you like your final financial destination to be? For example, where would you like to live, what type of home would you like to live in, what charities would you like to support, what schools would you like your children to attend?

_____

_____

_____

_____

_____

A-4

Celebrate!

1. How would you like to celebrate? What would be a small celebration for you?

_____

_____

_____

2. What would be a large celebration for you?

_____

_____

_____

_____

3. What celebration can you have right now that will help you acknowledge and congratulate yourself for the difficult work that you have done so far?

_____

_____

_____

_____

B-1

Your Assets

1. List your income sources. Include your salary, commissions, bonuses, etc.

    Income Type   **Amount**

    _____   _____

    _____   _____

    _____   _____

    _____   _____

                    Total   _____

2. List all of your financial assets. Consider such items as stocks, bonds, art, collectibles, cash, real estate, retirement accounts, etc.

Item   **Value**

_____   _____

_____   _____

_____   _____

_____   _____

_____   _____

_____   _____

                    Total   _____

3. List your intangible assets. This could include things like your desire for a better life, your courage, your determination, your family and friends, your health, your skills, etc.

_____

_____

_____

_____

_____

B-2

Debt Inventory Template

Creditor	Current Balance	Credit Limit	Available Credit	Interest Rate	Monthly Payment
				Totals	

B-3

Debt Inventory Sample

Creditor	Current Balance	Credit Limit	Available Credit	Interest Rate	Monthly Payment
Mortgage	$179,000	n/a	n/a	5.50%	$890
Auto Loan	$6,250	n/a	n/a	9%	$279
MBNA	$840	$1,500	$660	12%	$25
Capital One	$745	$1,800	$1055	13%	$15
Chase	$525	$2,200	$1675	17%	$19
	$187,360	$5,500	$3,390	Totals	$1228

C-1

Monthly Income and Tier 1 Expenses Template

Tier 1 Expenses

Monthly Expenses	Amount	Actual
Mortgage/Rent		
Food		
Clothing		
Auto loan		
Auto maintenance		
Auto fuel		
Child care		
Credit card 1		
Credit card 2		
Credit card 3		
Medical		
Auto insurance		
Life insurance		
House supplies		
Dry cleaning		
Contributions		
Allowance		
Home maintenance		
Utilities		
Totals		

Monthly Income

Income Type	Amount
Total	

Notes

C-2

Monthly Income and Tier 1 Expenses Sample

Tier 1 Expenses

Monthly Expenses	Amount	Actual
Mortgage/Rent	$890	
Food	$400	
Clothing	$100	
Auto loan	$279	
Auto maintenance	$75	
Auto fuel	$80	
Child care	$400	
Credit card 1	$25	
Credit card 2	$15	
Credit card 3	$19	
Medical	$40	
Auto insurance	$60	
Life insurance	$35	
House supplies	$100	
Dry cleaning	$15	
Contributions	$150	
Allowance	$50	
Home maintenance	$50	
Utilities	$145	
Totals		

Monthly Income

Income Type	Amount
Salary	$1872
Commissions	$2800
Bonus	$100
Dividends	$50
Total	$4,822

Notes

C-3

Tier 2 Expense Categories Template

Tier 2 Expense Categories

Overflow_____   Month:_____

Monthly Expenses	Amount	Percent	Notes
Vacation	$	%	
Recreation	$	%	
Allowance	$	%	
Entertainment	$	%	
Clothing	$	%	
Savings/Emergency	$	%	
Debt reduction	$	%	
Investments	$	%	
Gifts: birthdays, etc.	$	%	
Holiday gifts	$	%	
Contributions	$	%	
Taxes	$	%	
Auto replacement	$	%	
	$	%	
	$	%	
	$	%	
	$	%	
	$	%	
	$	%	
Total		%	

C-4

Tier 2 Expense Categories Sample

Tier 2 Expense Categories

Overflow____$1894_____   Month:__June_____

Monthly Expenses	Amount	Percent	Notes
Vacation	$189.40	10 %	
Recreation	$94.70	5 %	
Allowance	$94.70	5 %	
Entertainment	$94.70	5 %	
Clothing	$94.70	5 %	
Savings/Emergency	$189.40	10 %	
Debt reduction	$189.40	10 %	
Investments	$189.40	10 %	
Gifts: birthdays, etc.	$94.70	5 %	
Holiday gifts	$94.70	5 %	
Contributions	$189.40	10 %	
Taxes	$284.10	15 %	
Auto replacement	$ 94.70	5 %	
	$	%	
	$	%	
	$	%	
	$	%	
	$	%	
	$	%	
Total	$1,894	100 %	

D

You Are a Millionaire!

Did you know that you are a millionaire? Here is how much you will earn over your lifetime! Totals listed under Annual Income are Earned Income to Age 65. These amounts may be surprising, but by using the Spend & Grow Rich™ program, you will capitalize on this information and maximize your earned dollars.

Start Age Annual Income

Start Age	Annual Income			
	$25K	**$50K**	**100K**	**$150K**
25	$1 million	$2 million	$4 million	$6 million
35	$750k	$1.5 million	$3 million	$4.5 million
45	$500k	$1 million	$2 million	$3 million
55	$250k	$500k	$1 million	$1.5 million

About the Author

Gary C. Barnes combines a broad base of training and practice with depth of knowledge in the Financial Planning Field. He developed the Spend & Grow Rich™ Two-Tier Spending Plan™ during more than twenty-five years of experience helping individuals, couples, families, self-employed people, and corporations reach their financial goals.

His goal is to help people plan ahead so they have money when they need it most. He believes that adequate knowledge is an essential base from which to start. He has found that planning, discipline, determination and follow-through will carry a person or company to their goals.

Gary is a dynamic professional speaker who energizes and entertains his audiences. Almost without them knowing it, he also informs and instructs them on topics of building and keeping wealth, overcoming obstacles to achievement, and success. He gives keynotes and seminars locally, nationally and internationally to groups of 10 to 10,000 people.

Mr. Barnes provides high-performance business and sales coaching to help individuals and corporations take their businesses to the next level. He helps them develop plans that will help them meet their current needs and achieve their long term goals. His priority is to give quality service to his clients and to put his clients' needs foremost.

Gary Barnes is a leader in his field. He is known among his peers as the one to ask when they need to find solutions to complex situations. He is a Past President of the International Association for Financial Planners, Rocky Mountain Chapter. He is a Life Member of Who's Who National Registry for Financial Services. He is past member of the Denver Advisory Board for the Financial Management Group (FMG). He is a member in good standing with the National Council of Exchangers with Gold

Card Status. He is a Fellow in the Life Underwriters Training Council. To contact Gary for speaking engagements, keynotes, seminars, or other information call him at or 303-989-0066 or email Gary at Gary@GaryBarnesinternational.com.

A Note from Gary

I hope this book has helped you in your own personal journey. If you would like to share how this book as made a difference in your life, please write to me. I am always excited to read your personal stories. Send your letters or e-mails to:

Gary Barnes International
3500 S. Wadsworth Blvd.
Suite 203
Denver, CO 80235
e-mail: Gary@GaryBarnesInternational.com
website: www.GaryBarnesInternational.com

A possible next step with Gary

Gary has created a remarkable program called On a Purpose Results. The On Purpose Results E-Course is a 13-week course designed to give you the mindset tools and techniques to make you more flexible, more agile, more confident, and more successful.

It lets you "be your own coach." To have more fun with your business. To expand your mindset. And to make the world better while improving yourself. Go to www.onpurposeresults.com to learn more.

To your success!

If you enjoyed
Spend & Grow Rich
Gary Barnes is The Ideal Professional Speaker for Your Next Event!
"The Traction Coach"

Gary Barnes is an International Speaker as seen on ABC, CBS, NBC & FOX , will leave your audience laughing and learning. An author, business coach, and professional speaker for over 25 years, Gary's high energy and humor will entertain, inspire AND deliver a message that is dynamic, impactful and FUN! Gary uses the power of story to help his audiences take charge of their lives—to ignite their dreams and release their blocks so they can reach their own personal summits.

Gary believes anyone can lead an empowered life, no matter what their circumstances are. He has built three successful businesses from the ground up. He also understands dealing with adversity-he has fought life-threatening illness and won. He believes that your worst day is the day you meet the man or woman you could have been. It's a choice.

Gary's Most Requested Programs
(Engaging, Deeply Touching, Hilarious)

- **How a Beaver Saved My Life** – The Real Life Story of Adversity to Triumph
- **Take a Flying Leap** - How to Prosper in a Difficult Economy
- **Maximize Your Business Now** – with On Purpose Results!

If you would like to know more about booking Gary for a keynote, breakout or workshop, please contact our office by calling 303-989-0066.

You may also e-mail your questions to:
Info@GaryBarnesInternational.com.

Share This Book!

Quantity discounts of this book are available.
Call us for more information and a quotation.
Personalized autographed copies are also available.

www.ingramcontent.com/pod-product-compliance
Lightning Source LLC
Chambersburg PA
CBHW021118210326
41598CB00017B/1492